Poetics o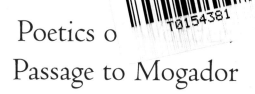
Passage to Mogador

Alberto Ruy-Sánchez

Translated by Rhonda Dahl Buchanan

WHITE PINE PRESS / BUFFALO, NEW YORK

This book was originally published in Mexico by Alfaguara.

Publication of this book was made possible by the support of the Program of Support for Translation (PROTRAD) with funds from Mexican cultural institutions (Esta publicación fue realizada con el estímulo del Programa de Apoyo a la Traducción (PROTRAD) dependiente de instituciones culturales mexicanas) and with public funds from the New York State Council on the Arts, a State Agency.

Translator's Acknowledgments: I am grateful for the support of the University of Louisville, which enabled me to consult with the author in Mexico. I would like to express my deep appreciation to Alberto Ruy-Sánchez for his assistance, support and friendship.

Printed and bound in the United States of America.

First Edition

Cover drawing: "A Pictish Woman." John White. Pen and brown ink and watercolor over graphite. c. 1585–1593. In the collection of the British Museum, London.

Library of Congress Control Number: 2013947486

ISBN: 978-1-935210-55-9

White Pine Press
P.O. Box 236, Buffalo, New York 14201

Poetics of Wonder:
Passage to Mogador

مَدِينَةُ آلعِشْقِ

For Elodie and Louis Santamaría,
with friendship renewed nine times over
in nine corners of the world.

Table of Contents

Preliminary Offering

Burning Words for Lovers

That moment had arrived when the lips of lovers ache from devouring each other, and even the touch of the wind reignites their senses.

At that hour, more than any other, words may be volatile sparks that, out of nowhere, perhaps from the air filling each vowel, rekindle the fire in their blood time and time again.

For lovers are as fragile as paper to the ardent caress of certain words.

Lovers gaze at each other with their fingers, but trace and touch one another with their mouths.

Lovers listen to each other even in their silence.

Lovers describe and reinvent one another, coining phrases that shine like new as they cross their lips.

The words of lovers are things, ethereal objects that suddenly flare and beat to the temperature and pulse of the body.

And then, from the table where they lingered before their first kiss and whetted their appetite for conversation, delighting tongues and palates, where hours before two mouths closed around a single fruit, from that table, the lovers took the word saffron and transformed it into yet another instrument for caressing each other.

Saffron: bound to the delicate pleasures of the palate and the enduring beauty of the Alhambra. Two dimensions of a culture devoted to the senses, that of ancient Al-Andalus, where the word was pronounced *Zaffaraán*.

Saffron, with its curved filaments, is an arabesque whose spiral comes from a flower and unravels in the mouth.

Their lips and fingers became stained with those blushing amber notes as they rode a wave of tiny kisses, pinching each other ever so slightly, just as they had seen the majestic purple flower gleaned in the fields, its three stigmas plucked by nimble fingers gathering the true red gold: saffron. Only three strands to each flower. And as it takes thousands to produce a few ounces, the lovers pinched each other in equal measure.

Saffron was and is the name of a treasure. But it is also known to be poisonous if consumed in excess. The most expensive and painful poison, although some would say the most delectable as well. Saffron overwhelms the senses, illuminating lovers as if they carried a sun within. Then it rises to the head, soon taking over the entire body, provoking neither hallucinations nor torment, but rather an excess of pleasure.

Even their gazes assumed a more radiant splendor from the word saffron. And wherever eyes, fingers, and lips lingered over the naked, beloved body, an ephemeral tattoo remained, a yellow or orange trail, visible only to the lovers for one meticulously prolonged instant.

They became tinged with burning desire for each other, and finally one of them made a colorful confession: "Your voice makes me feel saffronized."

With the chosen word, they were tracing a new map of love, an amazing geography of desire to tantalize their senses. And they continued their journey, unfolding and exploring "the saffron route" over their bodies.

From the same table, moments later they served themselves the word *aceite*, oil. One of the lovers, the smiling Hassiba, proposed it, evoking its Arabic origin as it slipped past her lips: *azzayt*. And the sound she uttered conjured the image of a small pitcher tipping its spout ever so slowly. The word spread, dense and fluid, smooth and mellow, and from its syllables there arose a fragrance that filled the air and attacked the tongue: pervasive but not sweet or salty. Oil.

Then they wished to intensify that rare sensation, and suddenly a special oil came to mind, one extracted from the fruit of the argan, a tree that grows at the edge of the Sahara. It is rather small, like a bush, but with very deep roots. Its bright green foliage stands out among the ochre hues of the desert, lending an air of mystery to the arid lands of northern Africa. It is a distant cousin of the *huizache* and *mezquite* trees whose semblance graces the deserts of northern Mexico. They are very ancient trees classified by scientists as "voracious" because their roots grow faster than their leaves and may become twenty times larger than their trunks and branches. Lovers dream of growing inside each other that way, with an excessive voraciousness to the twentieth degree, with a surging thirst in their most intimate veins, rendering them oil by the end of the day.

Argan oil is slightly darker and more golden than olive oil. It smells and tastes like its seed, known as "the nut of paradise," and leaves a fragrant sensation that scurries through the mouth and nestles unmistakably in the back of the palate. Some nomadic tribes consider this oil an aphrodisiac that arouses in those who taste it an immediate and persistent urge to make love. Oasis oil, oil of paradise.

By then the lovers felt the word oil was more than a taste upon their lips; a second skin, nearly transparent and liquid, coating the mouth ever so lightly and leaving a trace wherever kisses were planted.

Oil, with all its vowels, slithered down the skin of the neck. It mounted the muscles of the chest and circled the granular nipples, softening and stiffening at the same time all those obstinate and unbridled parts that tingle at the slightest touch.

Oil makes the hands sail as if blown by the wind and the skin feel caressed by what has yet to draw near: a breath, a shower, a presence.

Oil lulls and plummets, arousing lovers deep inside and inciting the darkest hunger of their flesh.

From that slippery lethargy, with lips ever more sensitive, Hassiba half-opened her eyes and slowly cast her gaze beyond the table, past the strands of saffron on the small blue ceramic plate, over the little pitcher of oil with the drop on its spout, above the bread crumbs and the glasses tinged with wine. She fixed her gaze on the fountain that trickled ever so softly against the wall, listening intently with her eyes.

From that fluid vision there sprang from her lips, clear and fresh as water, the word *zelije*, or *azulejo*, names for the finely glazed ceramic tiles covering the walls.

The lovers found themselves surrounded by hundreds of tiles, a geometric universe that dressed their skin with prismatic forms, casting naked reflections at the same time, like distorted images in an Impressionistic mirror. The room, patio, fountain, and columns formed one sensitive body of which they were now a part. A body made of light and colors: ceramic skin. A harmonious arrangement of modulating forms alternating between them and the world.

In the intense heat, the discovery of that cool skin awakened them to the contemplation of their new essence. They fell in love again with the marvelous composition that was transforming their loved one before their very eyes. Their hands were *zelijes* stirring the air with each movement. Their eyes *azulejos* reflecting their smiles. Their fingernails, fierce tiles digging into backs with a clamor.

Each part of their bodies changed into distinct geo-metric forms, pieces that fit together like the tiles on the fountain wall, creating a perfect abstract painting, an invitation for deep mutual exploration. And their gazes could now embark on an inner voyage, fervently touch-ing the fragile essence of the invisible. The word *azulejo* transformed them into an enraptured geometry.

They savored each word that rose to their mouths, sur-veying its depth with all their senses, prolonging each one in the body, until suddenly one of the chosen words appeared to be more tattooed than the others, filled with more meaning and mystery. And that word grew so much in their hands that it slipped between their fingers. It was made of water, smoke, light, and time. It was the word Mogador.

Another idea, I do not know which, made them think of Mogador and pronounce her name by chance, almost simultaneously. They came upon her by different paths, as if she were a part of the desired body that lovers can never resist.

It was the name of the port where Hassiba was born. And she thought, among other things, that Mogador was the culmination of the words that she and her lover had been relishing: oil, saffron, clay. Somnambulant words if ever there were any.

Like ghosts, there rose before her eyes the walls of Mogador, tinged the color of saffron, where they faced the ocean. Like other sleepwalking phantoms, scattered groves of argan trees came into view, beyond the ramparts, forming a sylvan necklace, a verdant wall uniting and separating Mogador from that other sea that is the desert. Finally, there crossed Hassiba's mind other slumbering spirits rising behind a veil of steam: the blue-tiled walls of the public bath, the *hammam*, the ritual center in Mogador of nearly all that concerns the body.

The word Mogador struck Hassiba's lover as an enormous mystery. Having never been there, it was not easy for him to understand his lover's fascination for her labyrinthine city, and yet, during restless nights, he had told Hassiba that whenever they made love, it felt as if he were visiting Mogador.

Naked amidst visions of saffron, oil, and tiles, he thought only of Mogador, his head filled with questions and vague images. But does Mogador really exist or, as some claim, is it the name of a woman described as a port? Why do they say she always seduces but can never be possessed completely? Why do they speak of her with wonder? Why do they call her the city of desire? Is it true they count by nines there because the number ten does not appeal to them?

And so, that afternoon at the edge of the sea, while the sky slowly turned a brilliant purple hue, Hassiba, grand gardener of Mogador, began to tell her lover, with captivating words, the things she knew about her city.

Although she did not mention it at that moment, the sunset hues reminded her of the remote origin of the city, when the neighboring islands were once called the Purpuraires. Indeed, they have been writing about Mogador since ancient times, many centuries before our era, when the Phoenicians invented an alphabet and writing, and settled on the Atlantic isle of Mogador. That is why some poets say Mogador is as old as the written word and the walled city is actually a letter of the alphabet that remained adrift, floating on the horizon.

The Phoenician alphabet, a unifying and practical force, reached the far corners of what was then their world, and later left its mark on the Greek alphabet, and on the Latin and Hebrew as well. Based on recent excavations, which unearthed some very beautiful ceramic pieces engraved with Punic or Phoenician characters, archeologists have been able to prove that Mogador is the farthest Phoenician port to the west of Carthage. Amazingly, their inscriptions reveal some stories about the city still told in the main square of Mogador, also known as the Square of the Snail.

It was because of a snail that thrives on its shores, that the fortune of this city began to be written and known around the world. The Purple Snail secretes a liquid that, before the invention of artificial dyes, was used to tint the most expensive fabrics in the world. And so, besides the beauty of the place, the Phoenicians found on this and other neighboring islands they also called the Purpuraires a natural dye that at the time was more valuable than gold. For many centuries, only emperors had the privilege of wearing purple tunics. They say an immense flag of that color waved over the most ancient wall of the port and was an extravagant and excessive luxury.

Many centuries later, the Romans circulated throughout their empire a book whose very scarce copies were so widely read and passed on by so many hands that unfortunately not one remains. They called it *De Re Mogadoriana*, which literally means *Things Concerning Mogador*. Supposedly, that book, also known at one time as *Poetics of Wonder*, was a primary influence on the work of Plinio Apuleyo, that Roman from northern Africa who traveled incessantly and made Carthage his home. He is the author of two essential Mogadorian books: *Discourse on Magic*, and more importantly, *Metamorphosis* or *The Golden Ass*, a tale considered to have had a profound influence, more than a thousand years later, on Cervantes, as well as Boccaccio. We can say that the imagination of both authors was sprinkled with a light dusting of Mogador.

Hassiba, who bore within her enough of that dust to form a large dune, knew better than anyone the purple trajectory of her city, for as a child she had extracted ink from the snails along its shoreline. With her hands stained purple once again, this time by the evening light, she began to thread for her lover the beads of her tale. A necklace of Mogadorian things emanating from her skin.

They are things of air, she told him: ideas, sudden revelations, repeated out loud for days on end, and later in dreams, night after night.

Things that take shape more freely in those transitional moments when one is neither asleep nor awake.

Things such as light lingering over dark skin, music in the folds of the body.

Things that sooner or later become songs, myths, tenacious fallacies, legends, poems of wonder, stories that contradict or complement each other. Or an occasional attempt at scientific hypothesis, equally debatable, of course.

Things that at one time comprised a book.

But no matter how much or how little is attributed to these things, we must remember they are merely what we make of them: stones in a river polished by the water of our hands.

These things, regarding what lies within and beyond the city walls, touch on nine themes that have captivated Mogadorians. They never cease to comment on the appearance of Mogador, making observations that are unique and contradictory, often probable or proven, but highly questionable or questioned.

Things like those told about the enigmatic and inde-scribable anatomic form, seemingly invisible but omnipresent, which the sex assumes in that capricious city fortified nine times over.

Slow or impetuous ways of relishing each moment of time within time; of writing history with clouds; of turning wind into light; of hearing with eyes and hands and seeing with ears the urgent yearnings of the flesh.

Things that run wild and free in the books of a library as if in a meadow. Things passed from one mouth to another, forming a perpetual spiral that retraces the streets of the port.

Together, these nine times nine uncertain things they say about Mogador (and a few others) show us perhaps a certain truth: they explain how and how much that phantasmagoric reality, known as the "city of desire," has grown in dreams and in the waking hours of those who know or envision her, becoming deeply rooted in more than one body.

As you read them, or listen to them (for it seems many have been told or sung in the main square of the port), let some of them grow and beat in your body. May these things multiply in you as they do in the body of Mogador. Because they are like restless seeds:

> Unknown fruits that enchant the palate,
> stubborn roots,
> rebellious rhizomes,
> thirsty stones in a dry river,
> fish sleeping against the current,
> still moving upstream,
> birds nesting and flying near the waves,
> trailing luster of vanishing stars,
> deep echoes of piercing sounds,
> endless moans of sighing lovers,
> ancient and pristine avalanches,
> fading footprints in the sand
> trampled by the zealous wind,
> images depicted by witnesses,
> passionate yet wisely skeptical,
> they are the whispers of those things

whose sex blossoms into murmurs
as they continue resonating
and growing into rumors:
they are words, these words.

I.

On the Appearance of Mogador

One

They say the city of Mogador does not exist, that she lives within us.

Two

But others insist she does exist precisely because she lives within us.

إِثْنَان

Three

Others, who appear to know much more, which always raises suspicion, claim that Mogador also exists on the Atlantic coast of North Africa, disguised, in more recent times, by an Arabic name to which some attribute magical powers: Essaouira. A name that should be pronounced quickly, as if the vowels barely exist in this word that always sounds surprising: "SsueiRA." A swift whistling name that has been given three meanings: the well-designed, the one of small walls, the city of desire.

Four

About the first meaning of Mogador-Essaouira, "the well-designed," they say the calligraphic labyrinth formed by her streets is another magical word, perfect in its geometric design, but unpronounceable by the human mouth. A divine word that can only be read and understood from the heavens. From Earth, it is merely obeyed, like destiny, like the attraction of the planets or the yearnings of the flesh.

Five

About the second meaning of the word Essaouira, "the one of small walls," I feel compelled to disagree and point out emphatically that her walls are not so small. From the desert or from the sea, they appear like giants defying the waves. But they embrace and harbor their city with such strength and protective sweetness that they diminish and ease the exaggerated concerns and anxieties of her inhabitants so that they may rejoice in the streets and in their houses. And this explains something often heard in Mogador: when they say her walls are small, they are not referring to their size but to the affection they feel for them. They are using a diminutive term of endearment to name them.

Six

For many reasonable and unreasonable arguments, she is also called "the city of desire," an idea supposedly invented by sailors longing for a welcoming port of call. Or perhaps it was created by those who navigate the other sea of Mogador, that of sand: by the caravans who cross the Sahara, also yearning for shelter and respite. And so, in both cases, she was present in the mind and body of those navigators of salt and sand long before she existed where we presently see her. Even now, when someone approaches her on their long journey, over waves or dunes, they always reinvent her.

Seven

They say that even before glimpsing her from the sea, with her dazzling walls speckled by crystalline salt, we recognize her initially on the skin because she is a city that touches us. At times, she does so abruptly, quite often imprinting the senses with a firm but delicate presence that leaves us struck by wonder, first in the eyes, then in the rest of the body, no more and no less powerfully inside than out.

Eight

They say upon seeing her, one cannot help feeling passionate about her, and as a consequence, falling madly in love with whomever is close at hand. They say lovers united this way never quarrel or separate, or suffer unrequited love. Discovering Mogador is a binding ritual.

Nine

But others say the only ones who can really see her, and only from afar, are those already hopelessly in love, or who at least feel the urgency of a desire that overwhelms them, burns them. They say that in an ancient language of the desert, the word Mogador means "the place where destiny appears": where the meaning of life suddenly becomes visible because it embodies an ardent desire for the other. They say that a rather indecipherable calligraphy, which the women of Mogador tattoo above the pubis, attests to this small fire that has consumed or transformed some love lives. This is how Mogador appears, behind the flame.

II.

On the Spiral and What Arises from It

Ten

Perhaps those who read these words, counting the cadence of their gaze, will have noticed or perhaps known for some time that in Mogador no one counts by tens but rather by nines. And though they are aware of the zero, they are reluctant to use it, letting it slip by in silence. They embrace the incomplete circle, the one that winds around itself before closing, drawing a spiral, the original figure of the very Arabic nine.

عَشَرَة

Eleven

They say that here the lines of life and desire advance spontaneously in the form of a spiral: that endless, lingering, capricious line, forever beginning anew. In Mogador, they do not consider life a peak to be scaled, as they do in other cities and cultures. The exclusive pinnacle of wealth and power, ultimate climax, rising success, and maximum fame enjoy no prestige here. On the contrary, anyone who thrives on the illusion of having risen to the top is said to have "fallen up."

Twelve

They say Mogadorians also speak in a spiraling manner, broaching or withholding what they want to say: very slowly, in a roundabout way. It is also said they approach places and objects in the same fashion, and this is why their streets are laid out like that winding spiral so inherent to their nature.

Thirteen

The Square of the Snail is known to be the heart of the spiral, where all stories, destinies, religions, virtues and defects, passions and desires are woven and tightly knotted. All those invisible strands of life are carried by the wind to the square. And it is up to each of us to unravel them, little by little, or at least try to decipher those that touch and guide us, even though it may be difficult.

Fourteen

And as evidence of that coiled presence of the invisible in the Square of the Snail, beating heart of Mogador, at certain hours, whirlwinds suddenly ascend. Even the wind finds in the spiral a form of sustained splendor.

Fifteen

They say that even in matters of business, Mogadorians follow this unwritten concentric rule that negotiates everything in a snail-like spiral. And they do so with politics as well, in a seemingly indirect and evasive way. Even their defensive and offensive military tactics rely on the principle of concentric castles that voraciously devour the enemy.

Sixteen

And naturally, the spiral reigns over all matters concerning love. For example, no one pursues an orgasm, that other discredited summit, which is why lovers happen upon it several times in each journey: whenever they embark inside each other toward a center that is always distant, but paradoxically also present, within reach. They say that Mogadorians make love as if wandering the streets of their city, and so they meander, always pretending to go astray. Over time, the expression used to describe someone who "wanders off," has become synonymous with "making love." And they say that each concentric stroll is unique: lovers are always surprised by something unexpected. Impassioned wonder is the essence of the spiral and desire.

Seventeen

They say that Mogadorians worship their gods with spiral devotion, aspiring to reach them by entering dwellings that shelter other dwellings, knowing that a direct approach is futile. They commune with their gods as they do with their lovers, slowly consuming themselves in the rings of their fire.

Eighteen

They say the fishermen of this port cast their nets in the form of a spiral, creating a submarine labyrinth where disoriented fish wander and stray, until, more entwined in their dreams than in knotted strings, they finally desire to be caught. In Mogador, it is believed that desirous fish taste better than those corralled. When taken from the sea in the traditional way, women detect an evasive look in their eyes and a taste they call the flavor of "anguished fish." Paradoxically, or perhaps because of the roundness of the spinning Earth, Mogadorians are considered very good, even outstanding sailors. They know that in this world, full of water and air and fire, the most direct line between two points of land is never straight.

III.
On Time in Mogador

Nineteen

They say that according to the calculations of the most ancient African astronomers, the sun slows down when it passes over Mogador, lingering there more than any other place on the planet. That is why time is measured here at a leisurely pace and things in the world are perceived differently, with a somewhat poignant intensity.

Twenty

Because time in Mogador passes differently under the sun than in the shade, and with even greater distinction from day to night, very infantile elders and extremely wise babies may cross our paths, as well as meticulous lovers who in the blink of an eye can cover an entire body with deep caresses and kisses that last a lifetime.

Twenty-one

Even the sand in the hourglasses falls differently here, at times very quickly and at others more restrained. It is believed that within each hourglass an inner wind controls the shifting sand of its small dunes, and that wise lovers acquire and cultivate a similar wind that guides all the movements of their body, in particular, making them slow the rhythm of their impetuous caresses.

Twenty-two

In Mogador, the heart is considered the most precise clock, or at least the most respected, and not just for its consistency, but also for its sensitive ability to distinguish the profound nuances of each instant: it is a clock that falls in love, becomes frightened, and moved. Its palpitations become milestones of life shared by two or more, and at times by all. The history of this city is measured by erratic hearts. The rhythm of blood in the veins, what one poet called "the music of the body," is like the national anthem for Mogadorians. And making love with a very erratic heart is how it is best interpreted and sung. Indeed, at official ceremonies, foreigners are shocked to hear the most patriotic Mogadorians nearly moan their anthem with an enthusiasm more amorous than warlike.

Twenty-three

Another clock that is quite respected in Mogador is the sea with her moving insistence. Waves rise and fall against the walls, embracing the city with a pervasive sensation of constant rhythm that touches everything. Moisture on skin and clothing, in books, nooks and crannies, and even the air, is in Mogador a clear measure of time. Here time is fluid. They say it quenches thirst and eases the penetrations of lovers. "Give love time," is a common expression, often uttered while making a gesture of spreading something, and accompanied by a smile that unfolds ever so slowly.

Twenty-four

In Mogador, lovers recognize the waves and tides as pendulums of that expansive clock of the sea, and as their city expands within that immense saline clock, desire incites them to caress bellies and backs like an undulating swell. And they enter each other like tides obeying the moon, embracing with enthusiasm the magnetic allure of the stars. Here, to love is to measure time.

"Let me touch your time with my hands," is a common but rather desperate saying, used to request an ardently desired intimacy. But if someone brashly tells a lover, "give me time," it is considered a blatant pornographic gesture. For some it is insulting, while others find it very exciting. Time in Mogador leaves no one indifferent.

Twenty-five

Singing and dancing is yet another way to measure time in Mogador. The heart is a bass drum or, if you prefer, castanets hidden deep beneath the skin. It is a kind of ritual guitar: the *gambri*, with strings like arteries. Time dances in the veins of lovers and expands its volume when the uncontainable blood swells the sexual organs. And it beats and beats reinventing the rhythm of the *clave* (one, two, three/one-two). They dance to measure scattered time, to discover it in the body of others, as in a shattered mirror. And, if everything falls into place with a certain grace and finesse, the moment arrives when the time of one is within the time of the other. And they say that a clock is within another clock when lovers are united and chime in unison to the beat of their hearts, as if dancing. But one must take care not to coincide with absolute precision, occupying the same fragment of time, for that is when time stops, like a heart stricken by a severe case of arrhythmia.

Twenty-six

Every day in the squares of Mogador, the story is told of a pair of clandestine lovers who began making love in an exceedingly rushed manner, beneath an old staircase in the market, under the shadow of an ephemeral wall of flour sacks. And when, with haste and reluctance to part, the couple finished their "quickie," more than twenty-seven years had past. Their respective spouses had remarried and their children had moved away. Unbeknownst to the lovers, who had never been detected, the flour that shielded them had become loaves of bread. "The inevitable occurred," says the storyteller of the Square of the Snail, "and it is not the first time this has happened in Mogador: the excessive impatience of those who desire burns the surface of time, which as everyone knows is smooth as silk, and lovers fall into one of the abysses of the calendar. The same kind of abyss of time that always leads us to believe, whenever we are making love, that only our love is eternal."

Twenty-seven

They say, with rhythmic insistence, that time in Mogador is another entrance to the body: an open and deep sex, a long good night, an appealing mystery. An apparition.

IV.
On the Mogadorian Light

Twenty-eight

They say that in Mogador windows devour the air with an enormous appetite, and that inside the rooms, all that air swallowed night and day becomes light. And from that splendor born of a voracious desire, pleasure unfolds in exquisite detail, as the light burrows under the skin, ever so softly and slowly. This is why Mogadorians say they were "touched by the air" when a brilliant idea occurs to them. And when a woman desires someone and that lust sparkles in her smiling eyes, they say she has "the look of air."

Twenty-nine

They say the opposite happens as well: light is converted to air, but naturally only during the day, when windows consume all the sunlight they can capture. Once inside the walls, light changes to air and circulates like the tender caress of a light breeze. Its golden presence warms the darkest corners of homes and the deepest folds of bodies in yearning. When the wind stops blowing in the port, they say "the air opened its dark mouth."

Thirty

And then both ways: air converted to light and sunbeams transformed into air fill the rooms of Mogador with a sense of plenitude that cannot be felt anywhere else. This abundant bliss is measured by a sudden smile that graces the faces of its inhabitants, indecipherable to outsiders. When light and air become a single substance that penetrates the body in an instant, the corners of their lips react by turning in a very precise manner. Only Mogadorians recognize that discreet yet expansive smile of plenitude.

Thirty-one

And tides of light, air, and plenitude flow over the bodies of lovers. This is why in Mogador the line where the back ends becomes deeper and scurries between the thighs. And when the wind blows over the walls of Mogador, breasts rise and buttocks tighten, testicles flaunt their glistening veins and the hair of the pubis becomes entangled when showered in light. And it is a mystery to me how the pubes with nary a hair appear disheveled under the flickering shadows and even the lines of their tattoos seem disoriented.

Thirty-two

They say candlelight has a force of gravity, and objects in the house may orbit around the flame if they are too light. They whirl so slowly that some people do not notice and come to the simple conclusion that disorder reigns over their lives. For some unknown reason, things turn counter clockwise. They say that it is the same force of attraction that hypnotizes those who happen to glance at a chimney, grill, or burning candles and cannot tear their gaze from the flames.

Thirty-three

They say that fireflies are confused with certain obsessive ideas and with the desire that shines in the eyes of sailors who have been at sea for a very long time. This is why in Mogador, from a distance, on the nights they land, sailors appear as a vibrant aura, a swarm of fireflies headed for the port.

Thirty-four

Lovers in Mogador collect those phosphorescent insects, which once illuminated the ancient reed beds of the port, and give them to each other as tokens of their eternal love because those winged beetles, commonly known as lightning bugs, are the only creatures whose amazing nocturnal glow continues to shine after death. And they grind the dried insects, mixing them with argan oil to form a paste that lovers spread over their lips as a discreet prelude to a kiss. Aphrodisiac powers are attributed to that "ointment of light." And in the darkest hours of night, it is always arousing to see that radiant trail left by our lips after traversing the body. They say that when lovers are filled to the brim with happiness, their bodies shimmer inside for days with a luster that betrays them, and even when they dress to conceal the intense light of their sex, the glow in their eyes gives them away. A well-known poem in Mogador relates how a lover nearly lost his sight when his beloved opened her legs and the dazzling splendor took him by surprise. Moved by the urgent desire to enter that light, he protected his eyes by appealing to all the senses so that he might gaze upon that luminous beauty with his hands, ears, nose, and tongue. They say the light in Mogador deeply transforms lovers in the same way, heightening all their senses.

Thirty-five

It is said that desire in the eyes of women (when they leave the *hamman*, the public bath, very relaxed) shines like the moon and illuminates all nakedness with extreme serenity. But it also kindles a strong magnetic force that attracts both men and women alike.

Thirty-six

They say that every other year, the windows of Mogador also devour all the light of the moon. Others insist that this is a false impression because it is from those windows that the eyes of women filled with desire illuminate everything that shines in the night, including the moon and the entire city. Likewise it is the women, not the moon, who deposit their gaze over the bronze skin of their lovers, casting their bodies in an ardent silver finish. And they do so with a delicate filigreed touch.

V.

On History and How it is Written

Thirty-seven

They say the History of Mogador is written in the clouds, which, as everyone knows, are in this city the most faithful reflection of what humans and some other mammals feel and have felt. The clouds are the inscription of the past, and at the same time, of the present. Like any other chronicle of History.

Thirty-eight

They say the History of Mogador is carried by the wind. This is why, when it is told or preserved in one form or another, they call it "cloud clippings."

Thirty-nine

They say the storytellers of the Square of the Snail are the primary "cloud clippers," but at times, women in wash houses and public ovens and baths, and even men sitting at café terraces in the afternoon practice this trade. Calligraphers draw clouds with such beautiful words that people contemplate them with delight, as if gazing at the sky or a fire, and they take great pride in their History.

Forty

History, or better said stories, are also preserved on embroidered fabrics whose geometric secrets are difficult for the uninitiated to decipher. They are "the fabrics of memory" and those who read them never tell the same story twice. This is why the people of Mogador have come to believe that the fabrics are alive. And that memory, like clouds, like History, never stops moving and adopting strange, incredible forms.

Forty-one

"The fabrics of memory" are small squares the size of napkins, measuring two hands on each side, which is why Mogadorians extend hospitality to visitors with the courteous expression, "History is in your hands," just as in other cultures they say, "make yourself at home." Each cloth features distinct geometric figures that form a colorful embroidered labyrinth. And, sewn on all four sides, are dangling strands of those shells that serve as coins in certain African villages. They say that recorded on those strands are memorable dates and census figures, but also the degree of pain during catastrophes and that of happiness during celebrations.

Forty-two

With those fabrics they often sew gorgeous caftans and *djellabas*, worn only at those special ceremonies worthy of "dressing in clouds" and cradling History in the wind.

Forty-three

They say in Mogador that when these fabric squares are piled together and sewn on one side, they are called "books." They say a few copies of those "books" exist, rather unfaithful but yet intriguing reproductions, drawn on parchment and embellished with metallic colors and the blood of heroes and lovers. And they say Mogadorians took the word "book" from a part of the cow's stomach that resembles pages, and that the Romans who lived in the neighboring city of Volubilis, near Meknes, were especially fond of that cut of meat and called it *librium*. After all, there are very close ties between eating and reading in Mogador, two acts that collate like the pages of a book.

Forty-four

In fact, they say, the librarians of Mogador classify History under the Kingdom of the Palate, alongside the section on Cuisine, and near the studies that identify winds by their salt content, and some chapters on the Art of Love, especially those describing lovers "eating" their partner's sex with great zeal. That classification implies that History is read with the entire body, each one interpreting it according to personal taste. And therefore History is a tremendous oral pleasure, more so for the tongue and lips than teeth. Indeed, History is always seasoned with the intimate and carnal touch of the one who creates the story as it unfolds, much to the delight of the listener's palate.

Forty-five

And, in every corner of Mogador, they say that people who listen to stories with lavish attention, with hypnotic fascination, are "eating clouds."

VI.

On Skin, its Mandates and Mutations

Forty-six

They say that all Mogadorians are born with their skin tattooed deep within, from the nail of their big toe to the last hair on their head. But that embedded inscription is so concealed, it can barely be seen and only rises to the surface by mistake as errant traces in the form of marks or moles on the skin of newborns. Midwives search for these with care and shout with joy whenever they find them, emitting that beautiful guttural ululation known as *youyou*. Birthmarks are signs that infants will survive "because they are calligraphed." They have a future, like nearly all Mogadorians who come into this world covered in small and large predictions and amulets. Hidden between their fingers and toes are also fragments of legends, love letters, and poems, many poems. And so each newborn assures the survival and creative renovation of traditions, of vital cultures and communal passions. And they also say, although with less certainty, that in some newborns one or more mythical novels may suddenly sprout under their nails.

Forty-seven

Not everyone is capable of reading all those inscriptions at first glance, but sooner or later, what is written on the skin reveals its force, its blessing or harmful presence. Nothing is known and nothing comes about that is not first written on the body. And although it is so important to read it, understanding all that the skin bears is very difficult. It remains one of the most vital and perplexing mysteries of the port. This is why in Mogador people look at each other so intently, whether up close or from a distance, when walking or standing still. They also search for stories in each other with their fingertips, those ten voracious readers. And greetings are always far more effusive than a regular handshake, with people touching necks and squeezing wrists enthusiastically.

Forty-eight

It is on the rough landscape of elbows, so they say, that one may feel the secret writing with greatest clarity, which is why it is common to see two people greet each other with an attentive gaze, a slight smile, and a mutual pinching of elbows. In Mogadorian families, good readers of elbows and knees are highly esteemed, as are the legendary "readers of scrotums and vaginal lips," who specialize in both "smooth and wrinkled" translations. The latter is a strange century-old profession in Mogador that is quite sophisticated. And though its practitioners are paid handsomely for their services, over the years they suffer from chronic back pain, failing eyesight, and insatiable thirst.

Forty-nine

All rituals in Mogador take into account that profound writing. Indeed, many are dedicated exclusively to reading and at times correcting or erasing what is inscribed beneath the skin. But also sheltered by the skin are predictions that seem indelible or have become indecipherable. "A stroke of luck," say certain wise women who prefer not to know what may harm them. Other women, stubborn optimists who hunger for good fortune and embrace life as an adventure, are more likely to be tempted by the pleasure of savoring and anticipating what may bring them happiness.

Fifty

When someone goes mad, they say certain lines of that concealed writing have converged, become entangled, or ventured where they do not belong. One possible cure is to write on the skin, this time with another kind of tattoo, one that can be seen and is normally created with henna. This exposed writing is always a passageway or window between the visible and the invisible, but it is not always possible to restore order to the underlying chaos. Quite often it is too late when the tattooers realize they have erred or gone too far. And that is when things risk going from bad to worse.

Fifty-one

Some insist that love is yet another form of lunacy, produced by erratic writing on the skin of the enraptured body, which creates the illusion that the entangled lines of lovers are merging toward a common vanishing point. And that serendipitous composition formed by the accidental converging of star-crossed lines is perceived by lovers as a "work of destiny." Those who try to soothe them, saying it is just a matter of perspective, are absolutely right.

Fifty-two

Midwives know that one can also read on the skin of newborns all the sounds their bodies will make in a lifetime, including strains of love, digestive laments, sighs, and smiles. That is why some midwives cover their ears when a baby comes into the world with tough and blotchy skin, covered in writing from head to toe. And in those cases of deafening clamor, all that will be imagined, including the most intimate desires, is also written.

Fifty-three

And what are those hushed sounds of desire, that insistent buzzing within the body, heard only by lovers? They say that its writing, its inscription, is the entire body in motion. Each body is like a somnambulant word that wanders, transforming itself with every step, every instant.

Fifty-four

They say the skin of animals also reveals their character and the sounds they make, but written in a different way. Silence lurks between the jaguar's spots, its stealthy presence soon disclosed by its ferocious growl. Birds display on their feathers a kind of score that makes them sing in a unique way instead of speaking. The ancient myths of Mogador, believed by all but taken literally by none, speak of men who sprouted feathers on their skin and were capable of seducing anyone they desired with their voice. But these same myths also speak of cunning men, with jaguar skin on their buttocks, treacherous scoundrels with whom it is advisable to proceed with caution, never turning your back or showing blatant availability for sex. Humans who feel that the animal burning inside them has surfaced to their skin. Although, perhaps, both humans and animals, sooner or later, share or will share that sensation. Because all of us carry an ardent animal within.

VII.

On Libraries and Those
Who Inhabit Them

Fifty-five

It stands to reason that the libraries of Mogador are evolving extensions of what has been inscribed on the skin of its inhabitants since ancient times. And it is no coincidence that tattooed hides protect the fragile parchment of books lining their shelves. Nor is it inconceivable that libraries and music share a common bond: their sheets are masterful metamorphoses of the skin.

Fifty-six

In Mogador, every open book is always ready to dance inside us. A blink of the eye or a brush of fingers over its pages is all it takes for it to penetrate us swiftly with joy. Once inside, each book meanders through the channels flowing within us and settles, in its own way, in unexpected regions of our flesh. In some they become discernible love handles around the waist, while in others they are converted to muscle, ready for action. And there is always someone who feels that books enhance their sex in thickness, finesse, and depth. In his indispensable *Anatomy of Melancholy*, the 17th century philosopher Robert Burton provides evidence that the consumption of many books may lead to reflective sadness. Their weight in the blood and the color of their ink increases black bile in avid readers, while the bile of those who limit their reading to only one book has a tendency to turn yellow, the bodily humor of anger, perhaps because they absorb more paper than ink. Quick-tempered dispositions nourish themselves exclusively with those unique books revered as sacred by certain vicious circles.

Fifty-seven

Each new book is considered a metaphor of a birth in Mogador. Or the announcement of the welcome arrival of a foreigner. And the quantity of volumes preserved in the city is always a multiple of the number of its inhabitants. This is why each day one of the librarian's greatest responsibilities is to maintain that precious proportion whose fluctuations are sensitive to increases and decreases in population, emigrations and wars, as well as euphoric reproduction and plagues.

Fifty-eight

The opposite calculation may also result: when a plague of moths or other insects enters the library and devours books, people consider this a bad omen, a sign of imminent wars or catastrophic epidemics. They say, with a bit of pride, and some chagrin, that Mogador is the only city in which many of the most tragic scenes of its History may be traced back to something that happened in the library.

Fifty-nine

They say that in certain enchanting sections of the library of Mogador, if two kindred books are left at night, side by side, three of them appear at dawn, and that librarians cultivate those "nights of blissful paper" like gardeners tend their flowers. And they take measures to prevent conflicts between opposing books. In the placement of books in the library, they aim to clarify that substantial differences may occupy the same shelf without necessarily sharing the same ideas.

Sixty

They say that healthy cultural promiscuity, and the natural hybridization among books, is quite apparent in the library of Mogador, whose strength stems from that incessant fertile diversity. At one extreme of the building, even the sacred books of Jewish, Christian, and Moslem faiths coexist by observing the art of distances, thus forming a perfect arrangement whose harmony can never be compromised by the fundamentalist prohibitions imposed by one hallowed book.

Sixty-one

They say the books in this library have very strange powers, and that whenever a book from Mogador is opened, somewhere in the universe a star explodes, or in northern Canada two hundred million butterflies begin their epic migration of three thousand miles to spend winter among the extinct volcanoes of Mexico, or the tides go out, or goats climb the argans, those Mogadorian trees that patiently guard the entrance to the Sahara, or in an attic of a forgotten corner of Bosnia-Herzegovina, a genius composes a symphony dedicated to the beautiful library of Sarajevo, destroyed in the war, or perhaps in a New York studio, a prolific Anglo-Mexican-Catalan sculptor engenders extraordinary bronze creatures: an amazing new species of *limulus*, those intriguing horseshoe crabs described by scientists as "living fossils," which openly defy Darwin's theories, having survived without changing or adapting for two hundred million years, and reproducing every spring on the beaches of New England and the peninsula of the Yucatán.

Sixty-two

Relegated to the shadowy corners of the library are certain books that no one in Mogador has dared to open for two centuries. An eerie glow emanates from them, seasoning the air with a luminous aura and filling the surroundings with the smell of sulfur. This has been going on since the last plague of locusts assaulted the city, consuming every living thing. After crossing the Sahara for several weeks with nothing to eat but themselves, Mogador was the first inhabited place they encountered, thirsty and ravenous. According to *The Concise and Abridged History of Saharan Migrations*, for the locusts as well, Mogador was and is the city of desire.

Sixty-three

They say that in Mogador books about animals, from the most ancient to the very modern and highly illustrated bestiaries, are kept in cabinets behind bars because at night beasts can be heard trotting through the books, from one side of the shelves to the other. Books on birds come unbound more quickly than others, making it necessary for their leaves to be sewn two or three times, while those concerning oceans and rivers are more often plagued by mold. Treatises on mining, such as the famous *Re Metalica*, are inclined to transform themselves into treasures, thus their study requires speculative readers who are somewhat miserly and unrelenting. The pages of adventure books turn faster than those of others. Invisible hands sprout from volumes of poetry, touching the reader deep inside the body. The pages of books on ethics, canonical law, and theology screech and their seams expand, at times concealing letters. Books by mystic authors open without anyone touching them. And those books regarding Mogador have the good fortune to be loved always with a passion that engages all the senses, with a growing adventurous desire, because, among other reasons, the books about Mogador extend far beyond their pages and continue writing themselves like dreams on the skin and flesh of those who read them, and even those who merely touch them. Perhaps without knowing it, those readers from long ago and those yet to come, are the ones who inhabit these books.

VIII.
On the Intrinsic Music of the Body

Sixty-four

They say that music in Mogador is a natural extension of the skin of its inhabitants, past and present, of their echoes in this world, of their harmonious and discordant notes, of their percussive outbursts and fugues, of their longing for the sun when it goes into hiding, and also of their joy when the moon rises. In Mogador, skin has an ancient name that means drum. It is said that many centuries ago, before a corpse was buried, they would make a drum with its skin. This would explain why the very ancient houses are filled with beloved little drums, hanging on their walls. People respect and cherish them and take them down to touch them as a way of remembering their deceased loved ones. They often place them exactly where the trade winds enter the city from the sea with a mighty force that shakes the drums, producing very faint and rhythmic low-pitched notes. For this reason, the first Elysian wind of the evening, which revives the drums of the departed, is called "Requiem Wind."

Sixty-five

But they also say that in spite of the importance given to the skin, it is the heart that is the most revered instrument of the city of Mogador, and that no one plays his own heart, only that of others, a fundamental law of the Mogadorian music of desire. And this is why it is an instrument played by at least two. What one person can do alone is dance to the rhythm of his or her heart when it is excited by someone far away. They have even gone so far as to assemble orchestras of the heart comprised of more than one hundred participants. And they also choreograph performances known as "Cordials," composed for the masses.

Sixty-six

The voices of Mogadorians are trained from infancy to imitate and enhance the flowing intonations of water in the fountains of the city. During adolescence, their voices can transcend any string instrument, including the finest violins. The obese train with the sea, chanting to it from the shore. The very slender with migrating birds that sing to the sun all day long as they flee the snows of the north. The elderly never stop learning to modulate their voices and are capable of producing notes audible only to themselves, sounds that travel not only through space but also time: "the sounds of the long shadows," "the music of nostalgia," from which surfaces, now and then, a joyful note, like a distracted smile at a wake.

Sixty-seven

Although music resounds in every corner of this port and along its winding streets, the music most cherished by all is that which is not heard but seen. Its harmonious composition is perfectly balanced and offers a dramatic horizon that nourishes the soul with its constant transformations. It is music for the eyes: the subtle yet deliberate sway of lovesick girls strolling very slowly; the daily symphony of hands exchanging money and objects in the market; the prolonged gesture of fishermen casting their nets and also repairing them with very nimble fingers. The alluring four-quarter pace of camels leading caravans into the city after crossing the Sahara loaded with salt from Timbuktu; the fluttering eyelashes of those contemplating the horizon from their windows above the city walls; the precise strokes of Mogadorian artists transferring a minute fraction of their weight from paintbrushes to damp canvases; the vigilant gaze of cats lying in wait atop roofs, towers, and rampart cornices; the gliding seagulls casting their shadows over rocking boats, and the perpetual and unrelenting sun setting below the horizon each day.

Sixty-eight

Noises of the digestive system, rigidly suppressed in other cities and cultures, are considered inevitable here. Mogadorians do not claim them to be music in its most rudimentary form, but neither do they negate their existence or ask others to pretend not to have them. Quite the contrary, they recognize and cultivate them like any other voice of the body. They are fine-tuned and reserved for an intimacy tempered by the tone of the existing relationship between the person who emits the sounds and the one who listens. Although there are no public concerts of them, Mogadorians learn to make music with those "noises" that in other cultures would only be perceived as offensive eruptions of the intestines. They are one of the symphonies of intimacy, little musical treasures of the body not meant to be shared and enjoyed with just anyone.

Sixty-nine

In the public baths of Mogador, they offer a type of massage called "instrumental," in which the body is the instrument that produces music. This can only happen once the steam has ridden the organism of all its brash toxins, the colored mud has stripped the dead cells from the skin, the black olive soap has renewed elasticity to all the tissues, and the aphrodisiacal perfume of the divine nut infusing the rare argan oil has penetrated even the imagination. Then it is time to be placed in the hands of the skilled masseuses who have studied techniques of orchestration with a master of this art and who play at least one other musical instrument beside the body. They know how to convert it into what is for them the quintessential instrument of all instruments, capable of producing the incomparable rhythms of the percussion box, the melodious strands of woodwinds, and the refined notes of the vocal chords. Playing the music of the body purifies us inside and out, preparing us for life, and also erotic love, which is the affirmation of life. It transforms us into something better than what we were before entwining our bodies with the vapors of those steamy capricious clouds that shape the silences of the *hamman* of Mogador.

Seventy

The sounds produced by bodies making love create the most sophisticated music of Mogador. The first time foreigners happen to hear their neighbors making love, they imagine cries of seabirds and thumping of drums arranged in bizarre harmony by some daring young composer. Others think of raging waves, and the throbbing drone of the *hajhuj*, or the clanging of metallic castanets, instruments played by the Gnawa musicians of Mogador to invoke spirits. In fact, they say that the music of Mogadorian lovers always invokes other bodies, and that is why behind the walls of Mogador the intimate solitude of lovers is always thought to be accompanied by another.

Seventy-one

They say that in the cellar of the main tower of the ramparts, there is an immense library of ancient scores written exclusively to be interpreted by lovers in the throes of passion. They show the infinite possibilities that may be explored by couples endowed with imagination and musical sensibility, and are regarded as more profound and provocative than any treatise on love, including the classifications of the *Kama Sutra*, which compared with these scores of desire, seem crude and limited. In Mogador, there is a long tradition of sophisticated melodious manuals that situate the act of making love very far from the shallow catalogues of contortions and much closer to choreography, the chant of the body.

Seventy-two

In Mogador, the music of the body is what distinguishes one person from another. There are people whose movements and sounds are aquatic in nature. They are capricious beings, elusive and desirable, who leave others with an unquenchable thirst. Others are quick-tempered and voracious like the music of fire, and close proximity to them makes the body sizzle, blaze, and burn. Then there are those with sluggish movements who sound as muddy as the earth. They are difficult to deal with and rarely expose themselves to intimacy, but when they choose to do so, they establish fertile relationships tempered by the cyclical seasons of the year. Others resonate so softly they seem almost ethereal. And though they are as lighthearted as a breath of fresh air, they may suddenly lose their composure, or simply vanish. By transforming themselves into the music of the four elements, riding the waves of their emotions, the people of Mogador become the constant reincarnation of the sky above their walls. It is believed that the skin of Mogadorians is comprised of the same four elements that form the cosmos, that the entire universe (which has borrowed the name of the tiny flower called Cosmos), is like a body itself, an infinite sphere of flesh and skin metaphorically created by sounds. That is the reason the skies over Mogador are viewed as an almost unimaginable entity, represented by beings who sound like water, earth, air and fire while they desire each other, while they attract or repulse one another. In Mogador, the music of the cosmos is the music of desire.

IX.

On the Capricious Nature
of Sexual Anatomy in Mogador

Seventy-three

They say that in Mogador bodies appear to be, at first glance, the same as in any other place in the world, but when viewed more closely, it is obvious they are quite different, even more so when the gaze is accompanied by feelings, that is to say, when one begins to fall under a spell, in which case distance is not a factor. Something happens that is far more remarkable than penetration or possession: the sexual organs in Mogador create an indescribable field of attraction around them that is beyond words, so much so that speaking of absolute magnetism or primal instinct does not even begin to describe it.

Seventy-four

In Mogador, when conversations about the body turn to the sexual organs, the mind skips erratically, affecting language as well, suddenly leading people to describe the invisible realm of the body and its intimate acts. The study of Mogadorian anatomy includes not only what cannot be touched or seen, but also what can be sensed, something that comes naturally there to the involuntary members of that caste known as "the somnambulants," a special group whose lives revolve around desire.

Seventy-five

That is why Mogadorians are perceived as very imaginative and even delirious whenever they speak of their sexual organs. But this is not because they wish to brag or flirt, or express false modesty. They do not boast about any exceptional attributes. Men and women simply think that the most important aspect of their genitals lies within the body, and what rises to the surface is a bit of capricious flesh that dangles or stands up straight, that blossoms voluptuously or withdraws into the shriveled folds of the skin. That is not the sexual organ, but merely its scab, its scar, a glimpse of the true sex that at times may occupy the entire body from within and subjugate all the other organs.

Seventy-six

They say the immense pleasure those minuscule parts may provide, compared with the boundless inner delirium that nourishes them, is like a mirage, a sign of something else, an indication that what is important lies much deeper and one must search for it with zeal in the body of the beloved. Those who understand that relationship the sex creates between the invisible and the visible have taken an important step toward happiness and becoming true somnambulants.

Seventy-seven

"They think only with their sex" is a saying in Mogador reserved for very few people and used to describe men or women with exceptionally brilliant minds and subtle intelligence who are open, perceptive, adventurous, lucid, and never selfish with their lovers.

Seventy-eight

In Mogador, no one speaks of the size of a man or woman's sex because even though that does matter, it is a question of something malleable that never ceases to change, always capable of surprising or disappointing. The size of the exterior sex is not a quality or designation, but rather a kind of impossible "anatomical verb" conjugated in very different ways by each lover.

Seventy-nine

Describing the sex of Mogadorians has always been a difficult undertaking, even for those who attempted to do so in anatomical treatises. Everything becomes confusing in the minds of those who claim to be experts on the subject. In their words, vaginas become flowers opening for the sun, dark images of hot and sultry nights, deep waters that disorient even the most experienced swimmers. Penises are confused with unbearable absences or tender words charged with meaning, with legs, arms, fingers or large noses, with strange puffs of air or trumpet notes in the body, or a cry bursting into a thousand pomegranate seeds, each a taste of infinite pleasure. Often the descriptions of the female sex are also used to speak of the masculine sex and vice versa. Although certainly these descriptions, which may seem somewhat imprecise to some, may actually portray in the most accurate and profound way the true anatomy of the Mogadorian.

Eighty

They say that in Mogador there are sexual organs that provide fulfillment to lovers even without penetration. And others that envelop and arouse with astonishing and unsettling perfection, without even the slightest touch. In this port, they refer to the sexual organs as a "somnambulant presence" or "phantoms of the flesh." This is how Mogadorians describe the undeniable reality of the invisible in matters of the heart, and it explains why they say desire, that mysterious and always surprising and charismatic master of transformations, is the real anatomy of the sex.

Eighty-one

In Mogador, the sexual organ considered the most obscene, powerful, and fundamental is the mouth. It unleashes passions, touches, moistens, bites, speaks. No other part of the body rivals its abilities to give and take, to discharge the most intimate of fears and the most spontaneous of pleasures. The mouth reigns over bodies making love, converting all else into metaphors, imitations, and images of itself. The most important things of this primordial port are born in the mouth and die there. This is why in Mogador words are considered the nucleus of the amorous act. They are treated with care, devoured with delight, treasured, and spoken with tenderness. Mogadorians know that sooner or later all the words in the mouth adopt or evoke the essence of the sex. And that is why it is through the mouth that one perceives, unites, and savors, nine times nine, the things of Mogador.

Loose Notes

Nine feathers,
from a bird perhaps,
and nine crumbs,
and nine currents of air
found later
beneath the manuscript
Poetics of Wonder.

In the libraries of Mogador the annotations found in the margins of old manuscripts or on the back of pages, papyrus, tablets, or scrolls are classified into three categories: feathers, crumbs, or winds. Ideas that discuss, explain, or question a text are called "feathers." They are ideas in flight, placed in the margins, in the air amidst key words. Conversations among birds. And it is well known that in Mogador the bird is a symbol of those who embark on a spiritual and sensual quest, and therefore a symbol of life in a state of desire. "Crumbs" is the word used to refer to comments that indicate or show the flavor a text introduces or leaves in the mouth of its readers. Unlike other cultures, in Mogador the tiny and fragmented character of the crumb is not in the least pejorative, rather quite the contrary. Mogadorians appreciate the allusive over the evident, the salacious over the unequivocal. And comments that seem more like impulses and energy, like forces that give meaning to a text, are called "winds."

Feathers:

1. Desire, a cosmos portrayed in Mogador with five colors or five elements: air, water, earth, fire, and the fifth essence, wonder.

2. The five books that form the *Quintet of Mogador* construct a Poetics of Wonder, a conception of the world based on the element of wonder. And that conception spirals, shaping each one of the books.

3. This book is the one that reveals the quintessence of the *Quintet of Mogador* and its exploration of desire, the axis of the spiral.

4. It is poetry, reflection and narration: myth and ritual that speaks at length about desire from desire and about wonder from wonder.

5. Nine times nine paragraphs form this book, a Vedic square with nine boxes on each side that offer an overview of the entire series of the *Quintet of Mogador,* built on the concept of the number nine as a framework through which all things may pass, a filigreed screen providing harmonious composition to everything.

6. In addition to the grid of nine times nine paragraphs that comprise this book, there is a prologue, a ritual to savor the words that give meaning to the life of the lovers and to show how the body that writes and

speaks is tattooed with words of desire.

7. The first three revelations of wonder: the epiphany or sudden **apparition** of Mogador, leads us to discover its unique **spiral** form as a counterpoint to the common perception of the world and an alternative to the concept of linear **time** that tries to impose itself on us as the only possibility.

8. Three other wondrous revelations: **light** alters substantially what it touches because it illuminates, in the deepest sense of the word, and therefore is the primary material of **History** and the stories of this place whose mutations and profound writings begin to surface and can be read on **skin** touched by the light.

9. A final trio of wonder: the pages of **books** that preserve what is written, are full of living beings whose bodies are sounds, composition, **music** of desire and music of the sexual organs that sing, primarily from the most obscene of all, the **mouth.**

Crumbs:

1. Oil.
2. Saffron.
3. Tile.
4. Skin.
5. Whirlwind.
6. Sand.
7. Light.
8. Letter.
9. Mouth.

فُتَاتٌ

Winds:

1. Tradewind, the one that comes from the sea.
2. Dunal, the one that comes from the desert.
3. Bilar, the one that comes from a sad soul.
4. Spiral, the one that creates whirlwinds.
5. Gullar, the one created by the fluttering wings of birds.
6. Sailar, the one created by sailboats entering the harbor.
7. Labial, the one that sings from the vertical lines of women.
8. Radial, the one that arises from the deep chant of men.
9. Axial, the one produced by the absolute intensity of desire.

The Creative Calligraphies of Caterina Camastra

A calligraphy accompanies each of the eighty-one texts that comprise the nine chapter of Poetics of Wonder. The following calligraphies appear on the pages that precede and follow the nine chapters:

City of Desire / 5   مَدِينَةُ العِشقِ

Words / 13, 27, and 142   كَلِماتْ

Saffron / 15   الزَّعْفَرانْ

Oil / 17   الزَّيتْ

Tile / 19   الزُّلَيجْ

Mogador / 21 and 23   مُجادور

Notes on the Author

Some rather strange things are said about Alberto Ruy-Sánchez, the supposed author of these pages: that he came to Mogador from an eastern Mexican desert and has never left because he discovered that there is a bit of that city everywhere. He believes that it is a dimension of human existence in which unbridled desire abides. He believes that Mogador resides in the body and that on clear days it is possible to glimpse its presence on the skin. Especially on the skin of readers of this book, and the others that comprise the *Quintet of Mogador*. *The Names of the Air (Los nombres del aire)* received in 1988 the distinguished Mexican literary prize, Premio Xavier Villarrutia. With this book the author began the poetic exploration of desire in narrative form, which continues with the novels: *On Lips of Water (En los labios del agua)*, which received the prestigious Prix des Trois Continents for its French edition; *The Secret Gardens of Mogador (Los jardines secretos de Mogador)*, recipient of the Premio Cálamo/La otra mirada in Spain; *The Hand of Fire (La mano del fuego: Un Kama Sutra Involuntario)*, and *Poetics of Wonder (Nueve veces el asombro)*. His work as a narrator, poet, and essayist include more than twenty titles, including: *The Demons of the Tongue (Los demonios de la lengua)*, *With Literature in the Body (Con la literatura en el cuerpo: histo-*

rias de literatura y melancolía), *In Praise of Insomnia (Elogio del Insomnio*, and *An Introduction to Octavio Paz (Una introducción a Octavio Paz)*, Premio José Fuentes Mares. His work has been translated to many languages and supported and recognized by the Guggenheim Foundation of New York, the Sistema Nacional de Creadores, the University of Louisville in Kentucky, Stanford University's Tinker Foundation in California, and the French government, which bestowed upon him the title of Officer of the Order of Arts and Letters. Since 1988, he has directed the editorial house Artes de México, and in 2006 he was awarded the Premio Juan Pablos al Mérito Editorial, the highest national distinction granted an editor in Mexico. He has presented conferences and readings in Europe, Africa, Asia and the Americas. Those who would like to know more about the author may visit his website: www.albertoruysanchez.com

Notes on the Translator

Rhonda Dahl Buchanan is a Professor of Spanish and Director of Latin American and Latino Studies at the University of Louisville. She is the recipient the 1993 President's Young Investigator's Award, the 2000 University of Louisville Distinguished Teaching Professor Award, the 2002 United Nations ASPIRE Multicultural Diversity Award, the 2004 University of Louisville's Trustees Award, and the University's 2011 Distinguished Service Award for Service to the Community. She is the author of numerous articles on contemporary Latin American writers, and is the editor of a book of critical essays, *El río de los sueños: Aproximaciones críticas a la obra de Ana María Shua* (2001). She has presented lectures in Argentina, Chile, Colombia, Cuba, France, Mexico, and the United States. Her translations include: *Limulus: Visions of a Living Fossil* by Brian Nissen and Alberto Ruy-Sánchez (Artes de México, 2004); *The Entre Ríos Trilogy: Three Novels by Perla Suez* (University of New Mexico Press, 2006); *Quick Fix: Sudden Fiction*, a bilingual illustrated anthology of short short stories by Ana María Shua (White Pine Press, 2008); and *The Secret Gardens of Mogador: Voices of the Earth* by Alberto Ruy-Sánchez (White Pine Press, 2009), which was supported by a 2006 National Endowment for the Arts Literature Fellowship and a 2004 award to participate in the International Banff Centre for Literary Translation Residency Program in Banff, Canada. In 2014, Texas Tech University Press published her translation *Dreaming of the Delta* by Perla Suez.

Notes on the Calligrapher

Caterina Camastra is Italian by birth and Mexican by choice. She is a translator, lecturer and researcher interested in Hispanic theatre history and folk literature. She has published articles in academic journals, such as *Vanderbilt e-Journal of Luso-Hispanic Studies*, *Revista de literaturas populares* and *La palabra y el hombre*, two award-winning children's books (*Ariles y más ariles: Los animales en el son jarocho* and *Fiestas del agua: Sones y leyendas de Tixtla*), and a number of translations of contemporary Mexican fiction for the Italian independent publisher BiblioFabbrica. She has given lectures and conferences in various Mexican cities, as well as in Cádiz in Spain, Faro in Portugal, and Rabat and Casablanca in Morocco. She fell in love with Arabic calligraphy because of Alberto Ruy-Sánchez's books and studied as an apprentice to the calligrapher Mohammed Faqir in Rabat.

COMPANIONS FOR THE JOURNEY SERIES

Inspirational work by well-known writers in a small-book format
designed to be carried along on your journey through life.

Volume 24
Poetics of Wonder: Passage to Mogdor
Alberto Ruy-Sánchez
Translated by Rhonda Dahl Buchanan
978-1-935210-55-9   156 PAGES $16.00

Volume 23
Searching for Guan Yin
Sarah E. Truman
978-1-935210-28-3   288 PAGES $16.00

Volume 22
Finding the Way Home
Poems of Awakening and Transformation
Edited by Dennis Maloney
978-1-935210-12-2   190 PAGES $16.00

Volume 21
What Happened Was . . .
On Writing Personal Essay and Memoir
Genie Zeiger
978-935210-04-7   106 PAGES $15.00

Volume 20
Mountain Tasting
Haiku and Journals of Santoka Taneda
Translated by John Stevens
978-1-935210-03-0   200 PAGES $16.00

Volume 19
Between the Floating Mist
Poems of Ryokan
Translated by Hide Oshiro and Dennis Maloney
978-1-935210-05-4   90 PAGES $14.00

Volume 18
Breaking the Willow
Poems of Parting, Exile, Separation and Retun
Translated by David Lunde
978-1-893996-95-3   96 PAGES $14.00

Volume 17
The Secret Gardens of Mogador
A Novel by Alberty Ruy-Sanchéz
Translated by Rhonda Dahl Buchanan
978-1-893996-99-1   240 PAGES $15.00

Volume 16
Majestic Nights
Love Poems of Bengali Women
Translated by Carolyne Wright and co-translators
978-1-893996-93-9   108 PAGES $15.00

Volume 15
Dropping the Bow
Poems from Ancient India
Translated by Andrew Schelling
978-1-893996-96-0   128 PAGES $15.00

Volume 2
There Is No Road: Proverbs by Antonio Machado
Translated by Mary G. Berg and Dennis Maloney
1-893996-66-2   118 PAGES $14.00

Volume 1
Wild Ways: Zen Poems of Ikkyu
Translated by John Stevens
1-893996-65-4   152 PAGES $14.00